# Object Lessons
# from Paper Projects

## Object Lessons Series

Bess, C. W., *Children's Object Sermons for the Seasons,* 1026-8

Bess, C. W., *Object-Centered Children's Sermons,* 0734-8

Bess, C. W., *Sparkling Object Sermons for Children,* 0824-7

Bess, C. W., & Roy DeBrand, *Bible-Centered Object Sermons for Children,* 0886-7

Biller, Tom & Martie, *Simple Object Lessons for Children,* 0793-3

Bruinsma, Sheryl, *Easy-to-Use Object Lessons,* 0832-8

Bruinsma, Sheryl, *More Object Lessons for Very Young Children,* 1075-6

Bruinsma, Sheryl, *New Object Lessons,* 0775-7

Bruinsma, Sheryl, *Object Lessons for Every Occasion,* 0994-4

Bruinsma, Sheryl, *Object Lessons for Family Devotions,* 5762-0

Bruinsma, Sheryl, *Object Lessons for Special Days,* 0920-0

Bruinsma, Sheryl, *Object Lessons for Very Young Children,* 0956-1

Bruinsma, Sheryl, *Object Lessons Using Children's Toys,* 5695-0

Claassen, David, *Object Lessons for a Year,* 2514-1

Connelly, H. W., *47 Object Lessons for Youth Programs,* 2314-9

Coombs, Robert, *Concise Object Sermons for Children,* 2541-9

Coombs, Robert, *Enlightening Object Lessons for Children,* 2567-2

Cooper, Charlotte, *50 Object Stories for Children,* 2523-0

Cross, Luther, *Easy Object Stories,* 2502-8

Cross, Luther, *Object Lessons for Children,* 2315-7

Cross, Luther, *Story Sermons for Children,* 2328-9

DeJonge, Joanne, *All-Occasion Object Lessons,* 5690-X

DeJonge, Joanne, *More Object Lessons from Nature,* 3004-8

DeJonge, Joanne, *Object Lessons from Nature,* 2989-9

DeJonge, Joanne, *Object Lessons from Pebbles and Paper Clips,* 5041-3

DeJonge, Joanne, *Object Lessons from Your Home and Yard,* 3026-9

Edstrom, Lois, *Contemporary Object Lessons for Children's Church,* 3432-9

Gebhardt, Richard, & Mark Armstrong, *Object Lessons from Science Experiments,* 3811-1

Godsey, Kyle, *Object Lessons about God,* 3841-3

Hendricks, William, *Object Lessons Based on Bible Characters,* 4373-5

Hendricks, William, & Merle Den Bleyker, *Object Lessons from Sports and Games,* 4134-1

Hendricks, William, & Merle Den Bleyker, *Object Lessons That Teach Bible Truths,* 4172-4

Loeks, Mary, *Object Lessons for Children's Worship,* 5584-9

McDonald, Roderick, *Successful Object Sermons,* 6270-5

Runk, Wesley, *Object Lessons from the Bible,* 7698-6

Squyres, Greg, *Simple Object Lessons for Young Children,* 8330-3

Sullivan, Jessie, *Object Lessons and Stories for Children's Church,* 8037-1

Sullivan, Jessie, *Object Lessons with Easy-to-Find Objects,* 8190-4

Trull, Joe, *40 Object Sermons for Children,* 8831-3

# Object Lessons from Paper Projects

## Sheryl Bruinsma

**Baker Books**

A Division of Baker Book House Co
Grand Rapids, Michigan 49516

© 1997 by Sheryl Bruinsma

Published by Baker Books
a division of Baker Book House Company
P.O. Box 6287, Grand Rapids, MI 49516-6287

Printed in the United States of America

**Library of Congress Cataloging-in-Publication Data**

Bruinsma, Sheryl.
    Object lessons from paper projects / Sheryl Bruinsma.
        p.      cm.
    ISBN 0-8010-5776-0 (pbk.)
    1. Paper work. 2. Object-teaching. 3. Christian education
of children. I. Title.
BV1535.9.P34B78         1997
268'.635—dc21                                    97-28456

For current information about all releases from Baker Book House, visit our web site:
                    http://www.bakerbooks.com

# Contents

## Special Occasions

# Using Object Lessons to Teach

Teaching children spiritual truths in these difficult times is a challenge. Using objects to teach has several advantages. They help hold a child's attention. They give a focus to the lesson. They give a child a familiar frame of reference to enable him or her to understand the concept being taught. Object lessons are like biblical parables—a time-tested teaching approach.

This book is unique in that it offers suggestions for projects that can be inexpensively made from paper and utilize readily available tools such as pens, pencils, crayons, paint, and glue. These lessons are written for use in a worship setting. The paper projects can be made by children, however, during Sunday school, children's church, or craft time. The projects can be taken home by the children to remind them of the lesson and to help them retell it. Parents can also do these projects at home with their children during a devotional time.

Each chapter contains an outline that gives an overview of the lesson. This helps a presenter locate an appropriate lesson and summarizes the lesson in a format that makes the material easier to remember. Introductory and concluding remarks are included as suggestions to help the presentation go smoothly.

When giving an object lesson, it is important to remember the ages and needs of the children. An enthusiastic presentation will help hold their attention, as will language that the children can understand. Be sure to stick to your point and don't get carried away by unimportant details. And enjoy the children. They are God's gift to us. For more complete information on how to give object lessons, see the enlarged section in my first book, *New Object Lessons for Children of All Ages.*

# Christian Living

# 1

# Be Careful Where You Go

**Objects:** Footprints

**Lesson:** God wants us to be careful where we go.

**Materials:** Different colored sheets of paper, one large piece of paper, pencil, scissors, glue

**Project:** Make footprints by tracing around the children's feet. Put footprints on one large piece of paper or let each child keep his or her own prints to take home. For a large group or church service, you may trace footprints ahead of time.

## Outline

*Introduce paper project:* I wonder where these footprints are going.
1. There are places God does not want your footprints to be.
2. There are good places to go and kind and loving things to do. God wants to find your footprints there.

*Conclusion:* If you always think about leaving real footprints behind, footprints that everyone will know are yours, you will be careful where you go.

I wonder where these footprints are going. *[Hold up footprints.]* Where do you think they are going?

We can only really see footprints when they are in snow or mud or when we trace them like we did today. However, when you walk somewhere, you leave invisible footprints. You know you have been there. God knows you have been there. Most likely other people know you have been there too.

Are there places where God would not want your feet to go? Are there places where your parents or teachers would not want your footprints to be found? Are there places that you would be ashamed of having been? Who can tell me where your footprints should not be found? Yes, your footprints should not be found anywhere your parents or teachers tell you not to go. Your footprints should not be going across a busy street, walking into a neighbor's house without permission, going too far down the sidewalk, running out of your neighborhood, sneaking away from your group, or going away with a stranger. Your footprints should not be anywhere you can get into trouble. If you left real footprints like these behind, would you do the things we just mentioned?

There are many good places for your feet to be. There are many kind and loving things that God wants your feet to take you to do. Where would you want your footprints to be found? I like to see many children's footprints in church. Good footprints are left by children helping their parents, being kind to their brothers and sisters, walking and talking with an older person, bringing a toy to a baby, chasing after a baby as he or she tries to run away, and carrying and bringing things for others. God wants to find your invisible footprints doing these things.

If you always think about leaving real footprints behind, footprints that everyone will know are yours, you will be careful where you go.

# 2

# God's Grace and Good Deeds

**Object:** A paper spring

**Lesson:** God's grace and your good works intertwine to give you a full or bouncy Christian life.

**Materials:** Two long strips of paper; tape, stapler, or glue

**Project:** Place the ends of two long paper strips together, one on top of the other, so that they form a right angle. Tape, staple, or glue the strips together. Fold the strip on the top down or away from you so that it is folded around the other strip. Do the same thing with the second strip. Continue folding away from you until both strips have been completely folded. Tape, staple, or glue the ends. When pinched together and released, the folded strips will bounce like a spring. The folding can be done as you talk.

## Outline

*Introduce paper project:* I have two strips of paper. Watch me as I fold one behind the other.

1. One strip is called "God's grace." Grace means that God loves me the way I am, forgives me, will take care of me, and some day will take me to be with him.

2. The other strip is called "good deeds." Good deeds are the good things I do to show God I love him.

3.  We need both God's grace and good deeds in our Christian lives.

*Conclusion:* By folding "God's grace" and "good deeds" together, I have added bounce or energy or joy to my Christian life.

I have two strips of paper. Watch me as I fold one behind the other.

The first strip is called "God's grace." Grace means that God loves me the way I am. He will forgive me when I say I am sorry. He will always take care of me. He will even love me when I act in an unlovable way. His grace or love is greater than anything I can do wrong. I do not have to earn his love. I simply need to love him back. I love him and trust him to take care of me and know that some day he will take me to be with him.

The second strip is called "good deeds." Good deeds are the things I do to help others. Because God loves me, I want to love other people. Because God helps me, I want to help other people. I will do as many good deeds as possible to show God I love him.

Both of these strips are necessary to make this paper spring. If I had only "God's grace," I might think that I could do any bad thing that came to my mind because God would forgive me anyway. If I had only "good deeds," I might spend so much of my time trying to do good deeds that I would not have time to do the important, ordinary things God wants me to do, like clean my house. Yes, I need them both.

By folding "God's grace" and "good deeds" together, I have added bounce or energy or joy to my Christian life.

# 3

# Be Willing to Serve

**Objects:** Handprints

**Lesson:** God wants us to be willing to serve. Size is not important.

**Materials:** Different colored sheets of paper, one large piece of paper, pencil, scissors, glue

**Project:** Draw around both hands of each child and cut out the tracings. Older children can cut them out themselves. This may be done ahead of time.

## Outline

*Introduce paper project:* Each of you has two paper hands just as you have two real hands.
1. Giving a hand means helping. Are you willing?
2. The size of the hand is not as important as the size of the heart.

*Conclusion:* You have given me a hand to show how we all can serve. You still have another hand to take home. Use it to remind you to give someone a hand.

Each of you has two paper hands just as you have two real hands. Who is willing to give me a hand? I will put one hand from each of you on this big piece of paper. *[If a child is not willing to part with a paper hand at this point, wait until the end of the lesson or let the child keep them both.]*

When I say, "Will you give me a hand?" I usually don't mean a paper hand. What do I usually mean? Yes, giving a hand means using your real hands to help. Are you willing to give me a hand if I need you to help me? If you could really see Jesus here in this room, would you be willing to help him? Jesus is here with us and he does want your help. He needs you to help his people. He wants you to be willing to use your hands to carry, to clean, to sort, to straighten, to put away, to hug, to hold someone's hand. Sometimes he wants your hands to be folded in prayer. Did you know that when your hands do something for someone, it is as if you did it for Jesus?

Look at the handprints on this piece of paper. They are different sizes, but they all have five fingers. They all work the same. The size of your hand is not as important as the size of your heart. A small hand can bring comfort just as well as a big hand if your heart is willing. A small hand can put away toys as well as a big hand if your heart is willing. A small hand can bring someone a book just as well as a big hand. Sometimes a small hand is just right.

You have given me a hand to show how we all can serve. You still have another hand to take home. Use it to remind you to give someone a hand.

# 4

# The Power of God's Love

**Objects:** Watercolors

**Lesson:** God's love is like the water that makes watercolors work.

**Materials:** Watercolors, paper, paint brushes

**Project:** Paint a picture following the intruction in the lesson.

## Outline

*Introduce paper project:* I'm ready to paint.

1. We need water to make watercolors work just as we need God's love to make the Christian life work.
2. Just as we can mix watercolors, God's love can mix and make something new.
3. God's love can blend very different people into Christians who care about each other.

*Conclusion:* I can't use these paints without water. I can't live a full, happy, colorful life without God's love.

I'm ready to paint. I'm going to use some green to make a bush. *[Try to use the paint without adding water.]* This isn't working. Something is wrong here. I've seen other people use these paints and they worked fine.

Who knows what my problem is? Why won't these watercolors work?

Yes, I need water. I guess that's why we call these paints watercolors. Let me put some water on them. *[Put water on and paint a picture.]* Yes, now they work fine. Trying to use watercolors without water is like trying to live a Christian life without God's love.

Pretend this water is God's love. I need God's love in my heart to help me love others *[dip brush into water]*. I need God's love in my heart to help me spread his message *[paint on paper]*. I need God's love to clean me and take away unkind thoughts and hurt feelings *[clean brush in water]*.

Now I want to use purple, but there isn't any purple. What can I do? Something else wonderful about God's love is that it can help mix and make something new. I can take this blue and some red and mix them, and I get purple. God can take my feelings of sadness or anger and mix them with his love until I become peaceful. God's love can make things into something new.

I can also blend with water. Let's pretend these stripes are three different people *[paint three stripes of different colors close together but not touching (yellow, orange, and red work well)]*. Now watch as I dip my brush into God's love and "paint" the water back and forth over the three colors. Look, the three "people" begin to share and care about each other. As they share in God's love, they become more like each other. God's love can blend very different people into Christians who care about each other.

I can't use these paints without water. I can't live a full, happy, colorful life without God's love.

# 5

# Sharing

**Object:** A torn paper design

**Lesson:** God wants us to share and make the world a better place.

**Materials:** Different colored sheets of paper, plain sheets of paper, glue

**Project:** Give each child a colored piece of paper and a plain sheet. Children will tear pieces from their colored paper and will give one to each of the other children to make a design.

## Outline

*Introduce paper project:* Today we are going to make a design with torn paper. If I used only one color, my design would be okay, but I know a way to make it much better.

1. If you all share your colors with me, I will have a more colorful design. God is happy when you share.

2. If you all share your colors with each other, everyone will have a more colorful design. God is happy when you share.

3. If someone has no color to give you back, will you share? God is happier when you share without expecting to get anything yourself. God is

happiest when you share something you would like to keep.

*Conclusion:* God wants us to share and make the world a better place.

Today we are going to make a design with torn paper. If I used only one color, my design would be okay, but I know a way to make it much better. Each of us has a piece of colored paper. If I tear off a piece of my colored paper and give it to you, will you give me a piece of yours? *[Each child gives you a piece in return for one of yours, or selected children give you one if you are in a large group or church service.]* I am gluing all your beautiful colors to my paper to make a colorful design. Thank you. I couldn't have done it without you. God is happy that you shared with me.

Now each of you has two colors, your own and the piece I gave you. How can you all have a more colorful design? Yes, you can share with each other. Are you willing to share with each other?

I have given out all the colors. What if someone new joined our group and didn't have a different color? Would you be willing to share with that person, even though that child did not have a color to give you? God is happy when you share willingly. He is happier if you share and do not want to get anything back. He is happier still when you give something you really wanted to keep.

God wants us to share and make the world a better place.

# Let Your Light Shine

**Objects:** Punched holes

**Lesson:** Give of yourself so that the light of Jesus can shine through you.

**Materials:** Hole punches, paper (small holes can also be cut out of the paper)

**Project:** Punch holes following the instructions in the lesson.

## Outline

*Introduce paper project:* Don't you just love to punch holes?

1. Punching out little pieces of the paper is like giving of ourselves in kindness to other people.
2. When we give of ourselves, the love of Jesus can shine through us. Others can see Jesus in us.

*Conclusion:* I like having Jesus' light shine through me.

**D**on't you just love to punch holes? Think of this paper as you, and the little pieces that are being punched out as kindnesses you do. You are giving of yourself to help other people. *[Continue punching holes as you talk.]* There goes a hug. These punched out pieces are smiles and kind words. This one is the book you shared with a friend. Here is a bag you carried for your mother. Punch, punch, punch! There are so many little ways we can make God's world a better place. Giving of ourselves is a wonderful thing to do. It can also be fun, because it makes us feel good that we helped someone.

Look what has happened to our piece of paper as we have been busy giving of ourselves. We have all these little holes in it. Watch what happens when I hold the paper up to the light. The light shines through the little holes. Think of that as the light of Jesus shining through us. If there were no holes in the paper, nobody could see the light of Jesus inside of us. But when we do things for other people, it shines through. Others can see Jesus in us. I like having Jesus' light shine through me.

7

# Be a Good Example

**Object:** A crayon rubbing

**Lesson:** God wants you to be a good example.

**Materials:** Paper, crayons, bumpy objects (anything that is flat enough to rub the crayon over but has enough texture to leave an impression such as leaves, cutouts, stencils, flat toys, even textured hymnals)

**Project:** Make a crayon rubbing following the instructions in the lesson.

## Outline

*Introduce paper project:* This is called crayon rubbing because I put the leaf under the paper and rub the side of a crayon over it.

1. What you do rubs off on your friends (negative actions).
2. God wants you to be a good example.
3. You can be a leader.

*Conclusion:* Being a good example is a big job.

This is called crayon rubbing because I put the leaf under the paper and rub the side of a crayon over it. Watch what happens. You can see what looks like the leaf coming out as I rub the crayon. Let's move the leaf over and try it with a different color.

Did you know that when your friends rub against you, you leave a little print on them? Think about it for a minute. What you do rubs off on your friends. If you run and chase and bump into things, they do this too. They follow your example. When you shout, they shout back. They follow your example. If you ride too far down the street, who is behind you? Your friend! It's a big responsibility having friends, especially younger friends who will do almost anything you do or suggest. You are their example. They follow you. What kind of an example do you want to be?

There are many ways that you can be a good example. What do you think God wants you to do? Yes, he wants you to be kind and helpful. There are many kind and helpful things you can do. When you take a few minutes to pick up your room, your friends see this. When you answer adults respectfully, your friends remember your behavior. When you pick up a book and read quietly, your friends want to do this too. When you share with your friends, they learn about sharing.

You don't have to lie there like the leaf to give an impression. You can be a leader. You can bring friends to church with you. You can suggest kind things to do. You can say, "Let's help." You might need to say, "Don't do that. It's dangerous." Being a good example is a big job.

# The Expanse of God's Love

**Object:** A paper loop

**Lesson:** God's love expands to fit our needs.

**Materials:** Two or three strips of paper about two inches wide, scissors, glue

**Project:** Glue the ends of the strips together so you have one long strip. Then take the two ends and, instead of gluing them for a regular loop, flip one of the ends over so there is a twist in the loop, and glue. When it comes time to cut the loop, make a slight fold where you want to start cutting and cut down the middle of the loop the long way.

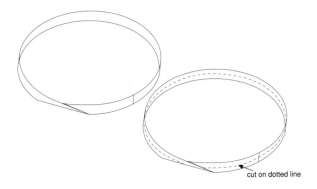

cut on dotted line

**Outline**

*Introduce paper project:* This is a special loop.

1. If this loop is God's love, do you think there is enough room in here for all of us and our needs?
2. When I cut this special loop, it doubles in size, showing us that there is more than enough room.
3. God's love is really bigger than we could ever imagine. It is big enough for the whole world.

*Conclusion:* God's love will always be enough for us.

This is a special loop. Before I do anything with it, I want you to think about God's love. Look at the inside of this loop. If this loop is God's love, do you think there is enough room in here for all of us and all the things for which we need God's love? This is a pretty big loop, but I wish I could make it bigger.

What would happen if I cut this loop in half? Would I have two loops? I'm going to make a little snip to give my scissors a place to start and then cut all the way around the loop. It looks like I might end up with two separate loops. What I really want is a bigger loop. One last snip and look at my loop. It is twice its original size. God's love is definitely big enough for all of us and all our needs and problems.

God's love is really much bigger than this loop. It is bigger than anyone could ever think of it being. It is big enough for the whole world. That means there is plenty of room for you and me in there. God's love will always be enough for us.

# 9

# Fellowship

**Objects:** Intertwining circles

**Lesson:** God created us to fellowship.

**Materials:** Paper, colored pencils or crayons, a compass or circular objects to trace around such as jar lids or paper cups

**Project:** Trace circles following the instructions in the lesson.

## Outline

*Introduce paper project:* We are going to trace around these circles with colored pencils.

1. We run out of room if we try to keep each circle separate.
2. Our design will look much better if we overlap the circles. God made us so that we live together, overlapping in fellowship.

*Conclusion:* I'm going to add more circles to my design. The more the merrier.

We are going to trace around these circles with colored pencils. *[Start out by drawing circles that do not overlap.]* I'm making a red circle here—that's me. Here is a green circle—that's Hailey *[fill in children's names].* The yellow circle in this corner is Sean. This purple circle is Megan. Pink is a good color for Christina. This blue circle is for Daniel. I'm running out of room. I wanted to put many more circles on this design. I know many more people. What can I do?

Nobody said the circles couldn't go over each other. I can still see the blue circle just fine when I overlap it with a yellow circle. In fact, it looks much better. We have discovered something that God planned all along. People don't live alone without touching other people's lives. If you lived completely alone, you would be very lonely. A little time to yourself now and then is a good thing, but I don't know anybody who is happy being alone all the time. Are you? I guess that is why it is punishment to be sent to your room. You have to be alone and can't join in with the family. School has "time out" for the same reason. We don't like to be separated from what is going on around us.

We have another name for enjoying being together. It is fellowship. Fellowship means there is joy in sharing God with other people. We laugh and talk and sing and hug and comfort each other. God wants us to do that. He made us so that fellowship would be a great joy to us. We have a lot of fun with each other.

I'm going to add more circles to my design. The more the merrier.

# 10
# Patience

**Object:** A picture to cut out

**Lesson:** God wants us to be patient.

**Materials:** A picture that is difficult to cut out (I use leftover flowered wallpaper), scissors

**Project:** Cut out a picture following the instructions in the lesson.

## Outline

*Introduce paper project:* There are some beautiful flowers on this wallpaper. I want to cut them out carefully.

    1. What is patience?

    2. Why do we need patience?

*Conclusion:* Let's all practice patience this week.

There are some beautiful flowers on this wallpaper. I want to cut them out carefully. I have to cut slowly. Whoops, I slipped and cut off a piece. I'll have to start again.

Do you know what this takes? It takes a lot of patience. What is patience? Patience means going slowly when you would like to go faster, like with this flower. Patience is being careful and taking longer so that you don't make a mistake, like with this flower. Patience is asking God for something and then waiting to get it. Patience is wanting to do something you are too young to do and waiting until you grow up more. Patience is wanting something very much but waiting for it instead of stomping around and grumbling and complaining because you do not have it yet.

Why do we need to have patience? We do not get everything we want when we want it. Sometimes we just have to wait for it. Sometimes we have to wait a long time for it. If we cannot wait patiently, we will whine and complain and get frustrated and make ourselves and those around us very unhappy. That is why we need patience. Sometimes we have to work very carefully and slowly so that we do not make mistakes. If we become impatient and hurry we might ruin what we are making or have to start again. That is why we need patience. If we want to help someone and it is taking a long time, we might give up, leaving the person feeling worse. That is why we need patience. God has many wonderful things in store for us, but we will not get them all if we are not willing to wait for them. That is why we need patience.

Let's all practice patience this week.

# 11

# Faith

**Objects:** Markers

**Lesson:** Faith is believing in God.

**Materials:** A set of markers, paper

**Project:** Use the markers following the instructions in the lesson.

## Outline

*Introduce paper project:* Today I am going to draw with markers.
1. Just as you believe there are markers in the box, faith means that you believe God exists.
2. Just as you believe a marker will write in the color it says, faith is believing God will be true to what he says.
3. These markers may dry out, but God will never run dry.

*Conclusion:* Don't let anyone or anything try to weaken your faith.

Today I am going to draw with markers. There is a reason I want to use markers. I want the markers to help me explain what we mean when we talk about faith.

Do you believe there are markers in the box? Faith means believing they are in here even though you can't see them. Faith also means you believe that God exists even though you can't actually see him. You believe God is real and you can feel happiness in your heart when you talk about God. You know he is real because people tell you about him.

When I take the cap off this marker, I can write with it. What color mark will this make? Yes, it is red *[make a red mark]*. It says red on the marker and the tip is red. It writes in red. Will it ever make a blue mark? No. God will also be true. He will do what he says. He will love you and take care of you. When you trust him to do what he says, you have faith. The more you learn about God, the more you know what he will do.

There could be a problem with these markers. What will happen to them if I forget to put the caps back on? Yes, they will dry out. Then they will no longer work. Will that happen with God? No, God will never dry out. He is always at work helping us and protecting us. Knowing and believing that is part of faith.

Do you believe in God? Then you have faith. As you grow older you want your faith to grow. Don't let anyone or anything try to weaken your faith.

# 12
# God Protects

**Object:** An envelope

**Lesson:** God encloses and protects us.

**Materials:** Envelope, paper, pencil, scissors, glue

**Project:** Make paper envelopes using a store-bought envelope as a pattern. Open all the sides carefully and trace around the pattern. Cut, fold, and glue the new envelope.

## Outline

*Introduce paper project:* We often make pictures or write notes to people. Where can we keep these things? Let's make an envelope.

1. What is an envelope? Something to surround and protect your paper just as God surrounds and protects us.
2. Why do we need an envelope? We need an envelope to protect things from getting damaged just as God keeps us safe from unkind things in the world.

*Conclusion:* Knowing that God protects us makes us feel safe and warm.

**W**e often make pictures or write notes to people. Where can we keep these things? Let's make an envelope. We only need one envelope from which to get a pattern. Then we can make as many envelopes as we need from plain paper.

What is an envelope? It is something that goes around our note or picture and protects it. Did you know that God fits perfectly around you? He wraps himself around you to give you courage, and he protects you from the bad things in life. We say that God envelopes you.

Why do we need an envelope? Well, what would happen to your picture if it fell on the floor and someone stepped on it? It could be ruined. Put it in an envelope and protect it. What if someone was rough with your picture and it began to tear? Put it in an envelope and keep it safe. What if someone spilled water on your picture? If it were in an envelope, you could take it out quickly before it got wet.

All of this talk about envelopes makes me very happy that God is our envelope. He will protect us from getting stepped on in life. He will comfort us when people try to tear at us or say unkind things to us. When unkindnesses are spilled on us, they will roll right off because we know that only God's kindnesses are important!

Knowing that God protects us makes us feel safe and warm.

# 13

# Self-Esteem

**Object:** A mask

**Lesson:** God made us who we are.

**Materials:** A paper plate and markers, or a brown grocery bag and scissors

**Project:** Make a mask by decorating a paper plate, or cut eyes, nose, and mouth out of a brown grocery bag

## Outline

*Introduce paper project:* I made a lion mask.

    1. Masks are fun to play with, but I'm not really a lion. I need to be myself.

    2. God made you, and you are special.

*Conclusion:* The next time you are unhappy about yourself, remember that God made you, and you are special.

I made a lion mask *[or make a mask of your own choosing].* Do I look like a lion? It is fun making masks, but it would be pretty silly if I tried to pretend that I was really a lion. My face looks a little like a pretend lion, but the rest of me looks like a teacher. I could pretend to be a pilot by making a pilot mask, but that wouldn't make me a pilot. You can't be something you are not.

You need to be honest about how you think and feel and what you can do. You need to be a real person who isn't afraid to be who you are. God wants us to be and act the way we really are.

God made the lion to be a lion. It is special. God made you special also. The way you smile, the way you walk, and the way you look are a few of the things God gave you so that you would be you and not somebody else. You are wonderful because God made you just the way you are. You are different because God does not make two people exactly alike.

The next time you are tempted to be something you are not, remember that God made you who you are. The next time you are unhappy about yourself, remember that God made you, and you are special.

# 14
# Join Hands

**Objects:** Paper dolls

**Lesson:** God wants us to join hands and support his work.

**Materials:** Paper, pencil, scissors

**Project:** To make a string of paper dolls, begin by folding a strip of paper accordion style to as many thicknesses as you can comfortably cut, usually six. Draw the shape of a person with the arms extending to the folds on both sides. Make the feet flat to the bottom of the paper so that the dolls can stand. Cut through all the thicknesses of the paper, tak-

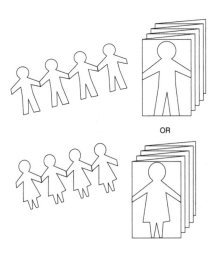

OR

ing care not to cut the ends of the arms at the fold. When the paper is opened, a string of attached dolls will emerge.

## Outline

*Introduce paper project:* I have cut out this paper doll. Now watch what happens when I open the paper.
1. The paper dolls are standing up. We need to stand up for what we believe.
2. They are hand in hand. We need to join hands and support God's work.
3. They will stand or fall together. We need to support our group.

*Conclusion:* Be willing to do your part.

I have cut out this paper doll *[leave paper folded]*. Now watch what happens when I open the paper. We have this little string of dolls hand in hand.

These little people can stand up *[hold them if there is a problem with them remaining upright by themselves]*. Many times in the Bible we are told to stand up for what we believe and for what is right. It is a good thing to learn to stand up for what is right while you are young. When someone is calling another person names, what should you do? Stand up and tell them to stop. When someone is telling a lie, what should you do? Stand up and tell them to tell the truth. When someone is swearing using God's name, what should you do? Stand up and tell them not to do this. When someone is littering or polluting, what should you do? Stand up and tell them to stop. When someone is in danger, what should you do? Stand up and help them. When you see or hear something that is wrong, stand up and try to change it.

These little people are standing hand in hand. It is often better when people stand together rather than alone. Many voices can be heard easier. Many hands can stop things faster. Many people can build or fix things better. When you join hands with others who feel as you do, more gets done. Are you willing to join a group that wants to make God's world a better place?

It is not possible for one of these dolls to fall without the others falling too. They stand or fall together. Your group needs you. It needs you to do your share. It needs you to be a kind and helpful part of your group. Would you want to be the one to fall down and make the whole group fall down *[demonstrate with the dolls]?*

Be willing to do your part.

# 15

# Forgiveness

**Object:** An eraser

**Lesson:** God want us to forgive others as he forgives us.

**Materials:** Paper, pencils, erasers

**Project:** Draw a picture following the instructions in the lesson.

## Outline

*Introduce paper project:* Before I paint a picture, I usually draw it in case I make a mistake.
1. Do you make mistakes? That's part of being human.
2. When you make a big mistake, you need a bigger "I'm sorry." Remember God will always forgive you.
3. Do other people make mistakes toward you? Will you forgive them?

*Conclusion:* Sometimes forgiving is harder to do than saying "I'm sorry."

**B**efore I paint a picture, I usually draw it in case I make a mistake *[draw a simple picture]*. What can I do if I want to change this drawing? I can erase it and change it.

Do you ever make mistakes? Of course, we all make mistakes. That's part of being human. It's part of learning. Can you imagine that some people get mad at themselves just because they make a mistake? We make mistakes in life. Why do you think we have the words "I'm sorry"?

What if I make a really big mistake? Could I erase a big part of the picture? Yes, if I do it carefully. What if you make a big mistake in life? What if you say or do something that a little "I'm sorry" isn't going to take care of? You can pray to God and ask him to forgive you. He promised us that he will forgive us and you can count on that. If what you did hurt another person, you can't always count on that person to be as forgiving. You need to give them a bigger "I'm sorry." You might say, "I'm really, really sorry. I didn't mean to do that. How can I make it up to you?"

What if somebody makes a big mistake toward you? What if somebody hits you or steals your toys? Are you going to listen to them when they say "I'm sorry"? Are you going to forgive them? You could just go on being angry. How would that make you feel? Not good! What would God want you to do? Yes, he would want you to forgive them. Sometimes forgiving is harder to do than saying "I'm sorry."

# 16

# Follow Good Examples

**Objects:** Stencils

**Lesson:** Follow good examples.

**Materials:** Stencils or cardboard shapes to trace around, pencil, paper

**Project:** Use stencils following the instructions in the lesson.

## Outline

*Introduce paper project:* I'm glad we have stencils because they make it easier to draw shapes.

1. Jesus is our best example.
2. God has given us great, famous people to follow.
3. There are many people around us who are good examples.

*Conclusion:* You just need to look for people who would be good examples and then decide you will use them as examples to follow.

I'm glad we have stencils because they make it easier to draw shapes. This stencil has many different animals. I think I'll try the horse *[or whatever shape you are using]*. Yes, it actually looks like a horse. I was smart to follow this stencil.

Just as I followed a good stencil to make this horse, God has many good examples for us to follow. Of course, the best example is Jesus. Jesus lived and talked and taught the people for years before he died for us. The Bible tells us about many things he did as an example for us. He helped people. He was kind to people and listened to them. He told people about God and prayed. If we are smart, we will try to live a life more like Jesus did. If we want our lives to look and feel like a Christian, we will follow his example.

God has given us other examples too. Some people give much of their time telling others about Jesus. Other people help the sick and those who feel bad. Many people give as much money as they can to God's work. People give of their energy to teach others. These people are good examples for us.

Look around you at the people you know. Are any of them good examples? How about the kind way in which your teacher always greets you? Is that a good example? How about the way your parents pray? Is that a good example? The people in the choir sing beautifully. Is that a good example? God has given you many good examples. You just need to look for people who would be good examples and then decide you will use them as examples to follow.

# 17
# God's Time

**Object:** A paper watch

**Lesson:** In God's time there is a season for everything.

**Materials:** Paper (stiff paper is better), scissors, pen or marker, glue

**Project:** Cut a strip of paper long enough to fit around your wrist and about the width of a watch band. Cut a circle for the watch face. Draw numbers on the face and attach it to the paper band.

## Outline

*Introduce paper project:* My paper watch has numbers, but it is not set to a specific time because I want it to remind me that in God's plan there is a time for all the events of our lives.

1. God has a time for you to be born, to live, and to die.
2. There is a time to work and a time to play, a time to have fun and a time to be serious.
3. There is a time to laugh and a time to cry. God gives you all of your emotions.

*Conclusion:* Right now is the time to sing and be happy and love God together.

**M**y paper watch has numbers, but it is not set to a specific time because I want it to remind me that in God's plan there is a time for all the events of our lives. There is a time to go to bed. What time do you go to bed? There is a time to eat our meals. There is a time to get up and get dressed in the morning. There is a time to take a nap.

When you think about your whole life, God also has a time. He has a time for you to be born. Do you know your birthday? There is a time for you to leave your parents' home and go out on your own, perhaps get married, get a job, have children. There is even a time for you to die, a time for you to leave this world and go to be with God.

We also say, "This is the time to . . ." Perhaps now is the time to play; later may be the time to be quiet. Now may be the time to have fun; later may be the time to be serious. There is a time to play games and a time to clean up. There is a time to work and a time to relax. If we do things during the right time, we and everyone around us will be happier.

There is also a time to sing and be happy and a time to be sad. If you were always happy, you would not need tears. Sometimes your life is serious, thoughtful, or quiet. Sometimes you feel upset or lonely or hurt. That is all part of God's time. God gave you all of your emotions. When you have sad times, God will help you. When those times are over, it feels so good to be happy again.

Right now is the time to sing and be happy and love God together.

# 18

# Giving of Yourself

**Objects:** Coupons

**Lesson:** Promising to do kind or helpful things is a loving and thoughtful gift to others.

**Materials:** Small pieces of paper, pen

**Project:** Write out coupons following the instructions in the lesson.

## Outline

*Introduce paper project:* I'm getting a gift ready for a friend.
1. Suggestions of what we can do to make someone else happy.
2. We should be willing to do kind things whenever another person needs them to be done.

*Conclusion:* Now that's a great gift.

I'm getting a gift ready for a friend. I want to give something special, something of myself. I will take a pile of these pieces of paper and write on them things I will do for my friend. On this one I will put, "This coupon is good for a cup of coffee and a chat whenever you need one." My friend will like that. I can also say, "I will baby-sit for your children while you go out whenever you like." This is a nice one: "Good for one cake for a birthday or whenever you want a treat." I will put these coupons into a card and give it to my friend for a birthday present.

What kinds of special things can you do for someone? First you need to think of who is going to get this gift. Perhaps it will be a birthday present, a Mother's Day or Father's Day present, a gift for a grandparent or aunt or uncle. Let's say you are going to give your mother a gift just to let her know how much you love her. Think about what you can put on the pieces of paper. Here are some suggestions: Good for a big hug. Good for ten kisses. Good for cleaning my room without complaining. Good for watching my little brother while you are busy. Good for my playing quietly for a whole hour. Good for doing a job around the house that is not my job. Good for singing you a song when you are sad. Can you think of other things you can do to make your mother happy?

When you give these to your mother, you need to be ready and willing to cash the coupons whenever she wants you to do so. You can't say, "Not right now, I'm busy." Being willing to do kind things is a good gift, but being willing and able to do them whenever your mother needs them done is great. It means you are really thinking of her before yourself. Now that's a great gift.

# Look Before You Leap

**Object:** Sunglasses

**Lesson:** Look before you leap.

**Materials:** A pair of sunglasses, paper, pencil, scissors

**Project:** Take a pair of sunglasses and trace around the face piece. Then roll the glasses to the side and trace the ear piece; repeat for the other side. Cut out the glasses, cut the centers from the eye pieces, and fold the ear pieces. You may trace and copy this pattern for the children if you so choose.

## Outline

*Introduce paper project:* Do you like these glasses?
1. Look before you leap.
2. Look for something good to do.
*Conclusion:* Let's all look for a place where we can make a difference.

Do you like these glasses? I can make them in different colors. If I drop them, they are not going to break.

Why do we use real glasses? Glasses help people see better. Some people wear glasses when they read. Some people wear glasses so that they can see faraway things more clearly. There are other reasons for needing glasses, but all glasses help people see better.

Even when we can see clearly, though, sometimes we do not really look. We do not pay attention to what is happening. There is an expression, "Look before you leap." This means that you look to see that there are no cars coming before you cross the road. You look to see that your father is going to catch you before you jump to him from the top bunk bed. This means that you will think before you act. You will stop and consider what you are about to do. You will ask yourself if it is a safe thing to do. You will think about whether it is a wise thing to do. You will wonder if it is something God would want you to do.

When we talk about looking and seeing, we also mean that we will look around us for good things to do. Do you look for ways to help someone? Are you looking for a person to comfort? Do you see a time when you can give a cheery word? Let's all look for a place where we can make a difference.

# 20

# Worship

**Objects:** Paper faces

**Lesson:** God wants us to worship.

**Materials:** Paper, pencil

**Project:** Draw a singing face (similar to a smiley face but with a big "O" for the mouth) and a praying face (a face with eyes and mouth closed).

## Outline

*Introduce paper project:* This is me. Can you tell what I am doing?

1. Singing is part of worship.
2. Talking about God is part of worship.
3. Praying is part of worship.

*Conclusion:* These things are good for us and God enjoys them.


This is me. *[Hold up the singing face.]* Can you tell what I am doing? I am singing loudly and joyfully. I love to sing.

Did you know God wants us to sing? He doesn't even care if we sing on pitch. The Bible tells us to "make a joyful noise." What kind of noises do you think God likes? He certainly likes the voices of people singing songs about how much we love him and how wonder-ful he is. That is an important part of worshiping him.

This picture could also be me talking about God to you. I probably do open my mouth this big. I want you all to hear me clearly. Part of worshiping is talking about God. You are worshiping when you listen to me and answer my questions.

*[Hold up the praying face.]* What do you think I am doing in this picture? I am praying. An important part of worship is closing our eyes and praying. Do you close your eyes and listen when we pray? Do you pray along when we say prayers together? Praying is talking to God. He likes it when we take the time to talk to him, to thank him for all the good things he gives us, and to ask him for what we need.

We do many things when we worship. We sing, pray, talk, and listen. These things are good for us and God enjoys them.

# Stay Close to the Light

**Object:** A traced picture

**Lesson:** We see ourselves more clearly when we are held up to the light of Jesus.

**Materials:** A picture to trace, paper, pencil, a window pane with light behind it

**Project:** Trace a picture following the instructions in the lesson.

## Outline

*Introduce paper project:* I want to trace this picture, but I can't see through this blank piece of paper well enough. What can I do?

1. Jesus is the light. He helps us see ourselves more clearly.
2. When we are closer to Jesus, we see him more clearly.
3. When we are closer to Jesus, we feel his warmth.

*Conclusion:* So, too, we become more like Jesus when we are closer to his light.

I want to trace this picture, but I can't see through this blank piece of paper well enough. What can I do?

I could set the papers side by side, look first at the picture and then look at the blank piece and make a mark.

Then look back again. This isn't working very well. There must be a better way. If I held this picture up to the light from the window, I could see through the top paper well enough to trace the picture. Do you see that? It works great.

The Bible tells us that Jesus is the light. He helps us see ourselves more clearly. We know that the more light we have, the better we can see. Just as we had to go over to the window to get closer to the light so we could see to trace our picture, so we need to get closer to Jesus so we can see ourselves better.

We could stand back and look at Jesus, try to be like him. Look again, try to be like him. Or we could move right over to him, stay close to him, and have him shine so brightly on us that everything is clear. When we are closer to Jesus, we see him more clearly. We know what is right. We know what to do. We get closer to Jesus by praying, singing, thinking about Jesus, and loving him with all our heart.

When we stand at the window to trace our picture on a sunny day, we feel the warmth of the sun coming through the window. In being close to Jesus, we feel his warmth. Jesus' love surrounds us and makes us feel safe and happy.

We get a much better copy of our picture when we hold it up to the light. So, too, we become more like Jesus when we are closer to his light.

# 22

# Joy in Giving

**Object:** Wrapping paper

**Lesson:** Christians find joy in giving gifts to others.

**Materials:** A large piece of paper, paint, household items that can be dipped in paint to make designs

**Project:** Make wrapping paper by using a large piece of paper (an open brown grocery bag will do or you can use the back of old Christmas wrapping paper if other large paper is not available) and paint. Paint can be applied in several different ways. Household utensils such as potato mashers, fork tines, and so on can be dipped in the paint. Designs can be cut out of halved potatoes for potato prints. Pieces of sponges make interesting prints.

## Outline

*Introduce paper project:* Have you ever made your own wrapping paper?
   1. There is joy in giving gifts to people.
   2. Making gifts is giving something of ourselves.
   3. It is also important to be a good gift-getter. If you are not excited about the gift, you can at least be thankful for the giver.
*Conclusion:* Consider your thankfulness your gift to the other person.

Have you ever made your own wrapping paper? It can be really fun. I made this piece of wrapping paper by drawing designs and sponging over them *[or describe your own technique]*. I will use this to wrap the next present I give. I like to make the gifts I give, but when I can't make the gift, I can make the wrapping paper.

Giving gifts is rewarding. I'm so glad God made us this way. He wants us to be generous and share and give things to people. I feel warm and joyful all over when I give someone a gift.

Making gifts to give is even more fun. When we spend time making a gift, or even the wrapping paper, we are giving of ourselves. We give our time, our thoughts, our energy to make something for someone. It is like giving that person a little piece of ourselves. God wants us to share ourselves with each other.

It is also important to be a good gift-getter. When someone gives you a gift, do you say, "I don't want that"? No, that would be unkind. If you are not excited about the gift, you can at least be thankful for the giver. You can appreciate the thought and the giving. You can sincerely and genuinely say thank you to the person because they have taken the time to give you a gift. They wanted to make you happy with the gift. Now it is your turn to give back to them the gift of happiness. Sometimes this is more difficult than giving a gift. Consider your thankfulness your gift to the other person.

# 23

# Christian Families

**Object:** A picture of a family

**Lesson:** God gave you your family.

**Materials:** Paper, pencils

**Project:** Draw a picture of your family. If time permits, give each child a piece of paper and ask the children to draw their family.

## Outline

*Introduce paper project:* I have drawn a picture of my family.

1. God gives you a family so you can take care of each other.
2. God gives you a family so you can share your life.
3. God gives you your family; you need to be kind to them.

*Conclusion:* Let's thank God for our families.

I have drawn a picture of my family. It is a big family now because most of our children are married and my husband and I have grandchildren *[describe your family]*. If I made this picture many years ago, it would be four children and a mother and father. That's still a big family.

God gave me the family I grew up in when I was young. I had a mother and father and two brothers. The parents took care of the children and the children watched out for each other. Is it that way in your family? Even if you have only one parent living with you, God has still given you this family to love and take care of. Do you love your family? Yes, even though sometimes we argue and fight, we still love our family.

Would you like to live in your house all by yourself? It would be scary and lonesome to be all alone day and night. I would not like it. I am so happy that God has given me a big family. Even the occasional unhappy noises are better than no noise at all. I thank God that I have my family to keep me company, to share my life.

God gives you your family. You do not look around and say, "That's a nice person. I'll take them into my family." You can't say, "I get along with this person. Let's have them be part of our family." You are born into your family, and it is your job to make your family as good as it can be. Kindness starts with you. You can't have an argument if nobody answers back. You can't have a fight if the person walks away. When you cheerfully talk to the members of your family, this cheerfulness spreads to them. When you are helpful and kind to those around you, they notice and begin to act the same way.

Let's thank God for our families.

24

# Ring Out God's Message

**Object:** A paper bell

**Lesson:** Ring out God's message.

**Materials:** A paper cup, string, an object that will serve as a clapper such as a bead or paper clip

**Project:** The easiest way to make a paper bell is to take a paper cup, punch a hole in the bottom, and string a bead or other small object inside for a clapper. Run the string through the top of the bell and tie a knot. Be sure to leave extra string for a handle.

## Outline

*Introduce paper project:* Can you pretend to hear the sound of this bell ringing?
1. God has chosen us to ring out his message.
2. We need to tell others about God.
3. A messenger for God will look kind and loving.
*Conclusion:* Are we all ready to be good messengers?

Can you pretend to hear the sound of this bell ringing? Ding, dong! It rings out for everyone to hear. You are God's bells. He has chosen you to ring out his message. He wants you to tell everyone about him. Are you willing to be God's bell?

A bell must have a clapper. The clapper is what bangs against the inside of the bell causing the ringing sound. A bell without a clapper has no message. People need a message as well. What will you say when you are God's bell? Will you tell people that God loves them? Will you tell them about the Bible? Will you tell them how wonderful it is to have Jesus in their lives?

If the string for the clapper is too long, the clapper will swing back and forth, but no message will be sounded. That is much like someone who is always talking but does not say much. God doesn't need just talkers. He needs someone who is willing to simply tell others about him. Because this is true, you can be a shy person and still be God's bell by letting your life do the talking for you.

My paper bell doesn't really ring, but it looks like a bell. Besides telling God's message, we need to look like messengers. A messenger for God looks friendly and acts kind and loving. If we talk about God's love but act mean, nobody will believe us.

Are we all ready to be good messengers?

# 25

# God's Beautiful World

**Objects:** Paper flowers

**Lesson:** God has given us a beautiful world. We must enjoy it and take care of it.

**Materials:** Colored paper; a straw, pipe cleaner, or coffee stirrer; scissors

**Project:** Draw paper flowers (a simple circle with five or six petals is fine). Make two small slits in the center of the flower and insert a straw, folded piece of green paper, pipe cleaner, or coffee stirrer. Leaves can be placed on the straw.

## Outline

*Introduce paper project:* These flowers remind me that God gave us a beautiful world.

1. The world is ours to enjoy.
2. The world reminds us of God's greatness.
3. The world is ours to take care of.

*Conclusion:* Then we and the people who live after us will all enjoy God's beautiful world.

These flowers remind me that God gave us a beautiful world. I love the colorful flowers. There are so many different kinds and sizes. I love to paint flowers. I love flower gardens and bouquets of flowers in the house. Flowers are just one of God's gifts to us. He gave us this whole big beautiful world full of animals, trees, clouds, stars, lakes, the sun, and many more wonderful things. God gave us this world to enjoy.

Do you like to stare at the clouds and see if you can recognize shapes in them? Do you like to smell the different flowers? Do you like to watch the birds fly from tree to tree and ruffle their feathers? Do you like to see squirrels chase each other around and around? Do you like to try to catch your shadow on a sunny day? Do you like to jump and splash in the water? All of these things are brought to you by your Father in heaven. Thank you, God.

Why do you think God put us in such a beautiful place? He could have given us a black and white world. We could have bare yards and fields. The world could be plain and uninteresting. Our God is not ordinary. Whatever he does is spectacular. He gave us this wonderful world because he is wonderful. He gave us this world so that we would recognize and remember his greatness every time we look at it.

Now that God has given us this beautiful world, what should we do with it? We can enjoy it fully. He wants us to do that. He also wants us to take care of it and not litter or pollute or ruin its beauty. Are you willing to do that? Are you willing to pick up after other people so that our world remains beautiful? Then we and the people who live after us will all enjoy God's beautiful world.

# Special Occasions

# 26
# A New Season

**Object:** A stack of paper strips

**Lesson:** There is strength in numbers. God wants us to stick together and support each other. (Children can use extra strips to make chains to take home and remind them that they are part of a team.)

**Materials:** A paper strip for each child (If there are few children, use thicker paper.)

**Project:** Tear the strips following the instructions in the lesson.

## Outline

*Introduce paper project:* Each of you has a strip of paper.
 1. A few strips can be torn quite easily.
 2. God wants everyone to do their part willingly.
*Conclusion:* That way we can make this the best season ever.

 Each of you has a strip of paper. Let's pretend it stands for you. This is our new season and there are many things to be done. I need a few volunteers to give me their strips. *[Take strips and stack them.]* If trouble comes along and tries to tear these strips, would they tear? May I try to tear your strips? *[Make small tear in the stack.]* Oh, yes, trouble has torn them. If trouble keeps on trying, the strips will be torn apart. What can I do?

I need more helpers. Who is willing to give me their strips? Will everyone pitch in and do their part? Thank you. *[Take strips and stack them with others.]* When I have all the strips together, do you think trouble will be able to hurt us? *[Try to tear the stack in another spot.]* No, nothing can hurt us if we stick together.

That is just what God wants us to do. He wants us all to help, to do our jobs, to be here when and where we are needed, to support each other, and to love him together. He wants us all to do these things willingly. As our new season begins, let's all remember that each one of us is important and we each need to do our part. That way we can make this the best season ever.

# 27

# New Year

**Objects:** New school supplies

**Lesson:** The new year represents a new beginning.

**Materials:** Several sheets of paper, new pencils that have been sharpened, new crayons

**Project:** Use the supplies following the instructions in the lesson.

## Outline

*Introduce paper project:* I have a pile of paper here. There is enough for everybody.

1. A new year is like clean paper. There are no mistakes on it. We can do whatever we want with it.
2. A new year is like a new pencil. There are messages to give.
3. A new year is like new crayons. They remind us to enjoy the beautiful, colorful objects in nature.

*Conclusion:* What will you do with your new year?

I have a pile of paper here. There is enough for everybody. What can we do with this paper? It is clean, good paper. We can do whatever we want with it.

A new year is much like this clean paper. Nobody has written on the paper. You have a new year to start fresh.

You haven't done anything with it. What will you do? Will it be something good? Are there kind and loving and good things you can think of for this new year? Do you want to be more helpful? Do you want to be a better brother or sister? Do you want to keep your toys picked up? Do you want to be cheerful and not whine or say bad things? Do you want to do your school work better? Do you want to pray and go to church more regularly?

A new year is much like a new pencil. It is sharpened and ready for me to begin. I like a new pencil. It reminds me that there are so many things yet to be written and messages to give. I can use a piece of this paper and write a note to a friend. I can leave a note for my family telling them how much I love them. I can draw a picture of happy people. I can draw some singing, smiling, worshiping faces. I can draw a whole line of people standing hand in hand.

New crayons also remind me of a new beginning, a new year, a new chance to do well. Crayons are also colorful. I can color my pictures. I can make trees and flowers and birds and other beautiful things God has given us in his world. In this new year, my new crayons will remind me how much I enjoy the wonderful, colorful things in nature.

I want this year to be a joyful, loving, Christ-centered year in which I can make others happy and share God's love with those around me.

What will you do with your new year?

# 28
# Epiphany

**Object:** A paper star

**Lesson:** The wise men followed a star. They searched for the baby. We too can follow the star.

**Materials:** Paper, scissors, pencil

**Project:** Paper stars can be made in several ways. Paper can be folded and cut (the six-pointed star of the snowflake without the cuts). Stars can be traced from cardboard shapes. They can be drawn free hand.

## Outline

*Introduce paper project:* I brought a star that I made.
1. The wise men followed the star (Epiphany). We follow Jesus too.
2. The wise men traveled a long way to find him. We can find him in our hearts.

*Conclusion:* When you find him in your heart, you are as happy as the wise men who traveled so far to find him.

I brought a star that I made. A star is much like the sun in the daytime sky. The difference is that stars seem smaller because they are farther away. You can see the faraway, white stars at night when the bright sun is gone and you look into the sky.

Who followed a star? Yes, the wise men. We call this day Epiphany because it is the time to remember the wise men who followed the star. The wise men were people who studied the stars. One day they saw something unusual in the sky that made them pack up and travel into the land of the Jews to find out about a special birth. A new and important person had been born. We don't have to look in the sky for a star to lead us to Jesus. We learn about him from our parents and teachers. If our hearts are open and we want to learn more about him, we are just like the wise men who searched for him so long ago.

The wise men had a long trip. They came from the East and had to travel on camels. Camels are usually very slow and not at all comfortable. When you make them run, you get bounced around so badly that you get bruises. I can't imagine that the wise men moved very fast on those camels. In fact, it took them about two years to find baby Jesus. He wasn't sleeping in the manger anymore then. He was living in a house. You too can find baby Jesus. He isn't in the manger anymore. He lives in God's house, in your house, and especially in your heart. And when you find him in your heart, you are as happy as the wise men who traveled so far to find him.

# 29

# Valentine's Day

**Objects:** Paper hearts with messages

**Lesson:** Love comes from the heart and is shared with others.

**Materials:** Paper (preferably red), scissors, pen or marker

**Project:** Cut out several heart shapes. Add messages following the instructions in the lesson.

## Outline

*Introduce paper project:* This heart shape stands for the heart that is pumping inside you.

1. A heart shape stands for love because love comes from the central, most necessary part of our body.
2. We give loving messages to share God's love.
3. Sign your name. The message comes from you.

*Conclusion:* It's like you speak from your heart to their heart.

This heart shape stands for the heart that is pumping inside you. Your heart doesn't look exactly like this paper heart, but everybody recognizes this as a heart. Right?

Why is the heart so important? Yes, it pumps your blood. In your blood is the food and oxygen your body needs. When a person's heart stops, we say that he or she is having a heart attack. You cannot live if your heart is not beating. This heart shape also stands for love. You cannot live a happy life without love. We say that love comes from the heart because the heart is the center of the body and is necessary for life. Love is the center and most important feeling. You cannot be happy without it. That is why God's love is so important.

Today we are going to make messages from the heart, messages of love, on a heart. We are going to share God's love. What messages can I write on my hearts? "I love you." That's the biggest part of the message. Now let's make these messages more personal. This one says, "Dear God, I love you. Thank you for loving me." Here's a good one, "Dear Mom, I love you. You take such good care of me." Do you like that one? How about this one, "Dear Dad, you are the best dad in the world. I love you"? There are all kinds of neat things we can say on our cards. "Dear Grandma, you are special. I love you." "Dear Grandpa, I love it when you play with me. I love you." "Dear teacher, you are special. I love you." What would you like your own messages to say?

After you write your messages or someone helps you write them, don't forget to sign your name. You want the people receiving the hearts to know that you love them and are thinking about them. You want them to know that the message came from your heart. People feel warm and loving when they receive a message of love. It's like you speak from your heart to their heart.

# 30
# Lent

**Objects:** Doors

**Lesson:** Lent is the time to prepare ourselves for Easter.

**Materials:** Paper, pencil, scissors, glue

**Project:** Holding the paper the long way, cut five doors (when started from the bottom of the paper, only the side and top need to be cut). On a separate piece of paper mark off the doorways. Draw objects in the doorways following the instructions in the lesson. If you wish, decorate the top sheet to look like a house. Glue top sheet over bottom sheet taking care not to glue the doors shut. The doors can be opened to reveal the objects drawn beneath in much the same way as an Advent calendar.

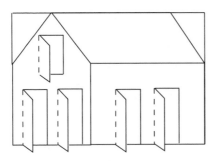

**Outline**

*Introduce paper project:* There is something behind each of these doors.

    1. Symbols to remind me of what Jesus did and ways to get my heart ready for Easter (cross, folded hands, Bible).

    2. Symbol of people to remind me to make sure my relationships with the people around me are good.

    3. Symbol of a heart to remind me to keep my heart clean and pure.

    4. Symbol of a thinking cap to remind me to think about doing all that God wants me to do.

*Conclusion:* Are you getting your heart and mind ready for Easter?

There is something behind each of these doors. I made this to remind me that this season called Lent is the time when we get ourselves ready for Easter.

Behind door number one I have a cross. What happened at Easter? Yes, Jesus died for us. We prepare for Easter by remembering what a wonderful thing Jesus did for us. Behind door number two I have a book and folded hands. This reminds me to read my Bible and pray as part of getting my heart ready to remember Easter the best way I can.

What is behind the next door? There are some people. This is a good time of the year to make sure everything is right between me and the people around me. Perhaps I need to say "I'm sorry" to some people. I want to celebrate Easter with a clean conscience.

Behind this door I have a heart. My heart needs to be right. This means I need to think about how to be more like Jesus. I want to be kind and loving. I want to consider the needs of others before my own. I need to think about Jesus first.

There is one more door here. Behind it there is a thinking cap. Well, this is what I think my thinking cap would look like. It reminds me that I need to think. I need to ask myself if I am doing all that God wants me to do. I need to think about how I can be the best Christian possible. I need to make sure I love God as much as possible.

Are you getting your heart and mind ready for Easter?

# 31

# Palm Sunday

**Object:** A paper hat

**Lesson:** On Palm Sunday we celebrate Jesus' entrance into Jerusalem. People thought he was coming to be king of Israel, but he was coming to be king of their hearts and lives.

**Materials:** Newspaper; or paper plate and string, ribbon, or yarn; or paper, scissors, glue

**Project:** Paper hats can be made from newspaper. Fold a page in half, fold down the corners in a triangular shape, and fold up a strip along the bottom on both sides. String, ribbon, or yarn can be attached to paper plates and tied under the chin. Hats can also be made by attaching shapes of hats to a band that fits around the head.

## Outline

*Introduce paper project:* In Jerusalem almost two thousand years ago, a crowd was waving palm branches and shouting about Jesus becoming king.

    1. We use hats to celebrate just as the people in Jerusalem used palm branches.

    2. We can join in their enthusiasm by shouting to and welcoming Jesus.

*Conclusion:* He was coming to Jerusalem to die for us so that he could be king of our hearts and our lives forever. We will use this party hat to remind us that we have a lot to celebrate.

In Jerusalem almost two thousand years ago, a crowd was waving palm branches and shouting about Jesus becoming king. We don't have palm branches. I have a party hat instead. Both are used for celebrating. The people long ago were waving their palm branches at Jesus in excitement and talking about the wonderful things he had done. They were singing and shouting and calling to him. Pretend that you see Jesus coming. He is riding on a donkey and everyone is shouting, "Welcome to the king!" "Isn't he wonderful?" "Look, here he comes!" "I heard he can heal people!" "Do you think we can get closer to him?" "Welcome, Jesus!" "Hail to the King!" "Yeah, Jesus!"

We should be even more excited. Those people thought they were getting a new king for their country. We know that Jesus was much more important than that. He was coming to Jerusalem to die for us so that he could be king of our hearts and our lives forever. We will use this party hat to remind us that we have a lot to celebrate.

# 32

# Good Friday

**Object:** A folding paper cross

**Lesson:** Jesus died on the cross but rose to give us eternal life.

**Materials:** Paper, pencil, ruler, scissors

**Project:** Make a cross that is five squares high and three squares across. The size of the squares will be determined by the size cross you want or the size paper available. Mark the squares so that the cross can be folded into a box. Cut out the cross. Fold it during the lesson.

## Outline

*Introduce paper project:* I made a cross out of paper. Who can tell me the importance of a cross?

1. Jesus died on a cross.
2. He was laid in a tomb.
3. He arose and the tomb is empty.

*Conclusion:* There is no one on the cross *[straighten cross]* and no one in the tomb *[fold into box]* because Jesus is alive.

I made a cross out of paper. Who can tell me the importance of a cross? Something happened on a cross a long time ago. Yes, Jesus died for us. He carried a heavy wooden cross through the streets of Jerusalem. Then the soldiers nailed his hands and feet to the cross and set it in a hole so that it would stand up. He hung there until he died.

Then a man named Joseph of Arimathea took Jesus down from the cross and carried him to a tomb, which was like a box carved out of a stone hill. I have a little box here *[fold up cross into a box and hold it closed]*. He put Jesus inside, rolled a big stone in front of the door, and went home. The next day some women came to take care of Jesus' body. When they got to the tomb, they found the stone rolled away and the tomb empty *[open up box and show that it is empty]*.

Now where do you suppose Jesus was? Was he back on the cross? No, once Jesus died for us, he was finished dying. He had risen. He is God's Son. He didn't have to stay dead.

Some people have pictures of Jesus on the cross so they will remember Jesus died for them. I like to see an empty cross like this one. There is no one on the cross *[straighten cross]* and no one in the tomb *[fold into box]* because Jesus is alive.

# 33

# Easter

**Objects:** A paper basket and eggs

**Lesson:** Easter is a celebration of life because Jesus arose from the dead.

**Materials:** Colored paper, scissors, stapler

**Project:** Make a paper basket using a piece of construction paper. Fold all sides in about two inches. Cut the two short folds on the top and bottom of the paper. Overlap in basket shape and staple. Cut a generous paper handle that can be doubled for strength. The size of the basket can be changed by decreasing the size of the paper and/or increasing the size of the sides. Cut many egg shapes by cutting through several thicknesses at once. Write messages on them following the instructions in the lesson.

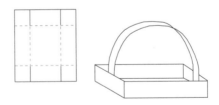

## Outline

*Introduce paper project:* I made a paper basket to carry paper eggs.

    1. Eggs represent new life.

2. My paper eggs have special messages.
3. I can share my eggs with you as we share the joy of this day.

*Conclusion:* I'll keep the rest of my eggs in this basket to remind me that Easter is a special day.

I made a paper basket to carry paper eggs. It's a good thing I made a basket because my eggs would be all over the place by now if I hadn't. I know why I have a basket—to carry the eggs. But why do I have eggs?

This is Easter, the time when we remember Jesus is alive. He has risen from the grave. We celebrate life. We use eggs to celebrate life because many forms of life come from eggs: baby chickens, baby turkeys, baby ducks, baby birds, baby fish, baby turtles. That is why eggs are important at Easter.

We do many things with eggs. We blow out the inside so we can save them. We color them. We decorate them in many different ways. We give them to people. We hunt for them. And we eat them.

The eggs I have made are decorated. They are not good for eating, but they are good for giving away because they have little messages on them. This one says, "God loves you." Here's one, "Easter is a happy day." Another says, "Jesus died for you." Some others say, "You are special," "I'm glad you are my friend," "I love your smile." I can share my eggs with you as we share the joy of this day. I'll give each of you one. I'll keep the rest of my eggs in this basket to remind me that Easter is a special day.

# 34

# Pentecost

**Object:** Confetti

**Lesson:** The powerful Holy Spirit, which sounded like a mighty rushing wind, descended at Pentecost.

**Materials:** Paper, hole puncher, a large box, a hand-held fan

**Project:** Punch out little pieces of confetti with a hole puncher and put the confetti in a large box.

## Outline

*Introduce paper project:* I like making confetti.

1. The powerful Holy Spirit came with the sound of a mighty rushing wind *[fan the confetti]*.
2. The Holy Spirit gives us love, joy, peace, patience, kindness, goodness, faithfulness, humility, and self-control.

*Conclusion:* I am thankful for the Holy Spirit.

I like making confetti. I like punching out all these little pieces. I made a nice pile of confetti.

Why do you think I made this confetti? Yes, it is fun. We often throw confetti to celebrate events such as when someone wins an important game. Today we are celebrating Pentecost. We are not going to throw this confetti, however. I would like to keep it in this big box.

Pentecost is the time when the Holy Spirit came to the apostles a long time ago. The Holy Spirit came with the sound of a mighty rushing wind. I can make a wind, even though it is not mighty or rushing *[fan the confetti]*. Pretend each of these little pieces of confetti is a person and look what happens when I fan them. Look at them run all over the box. They are tumbling up and down and acting a little crazy. The apostles acted a little crazy too. They became very excited. They began speaking in different languages. How exciting it must have been.

The power of the Holy Spirit is still with us. It is not like a rushing wind anymore. It is more like something we feel in our hearts. It brings us love, joy, peace, patience, kindness, goodness, faithfulness, humility, and self-control. It helps us to be helpful. Right now I need you to be helpful because some of our confetti people were knocked to the floor. Who will help me pick them up?

I am thankful for the Holy Spirit.

# 35

# Thanksgiving

**Object:** A paper plate covered with pictures of your favorite foods

**Lesson:** Thanksgiving is a time to say thank you to God.

**Materials:** A paper plate, crayons or markers to draw with or magazine pictures to cut out and paste onto the paper plate

**Project:** Prepare a paper plate ahead of time covered with pictures of your favorite foods.

## Outline

*Introduce paper project:* This is a plate of my favorite foods.

1. We are thankful that we can have our favorite foods often.
2. We are also thankful for our parents, brothers and sisters, homes, clothing, toys, and so on.

*Conclusion:* Let us say thank you to God for all the things he has given us that make us healthy and happy.

This is a plate of my favorite foods. *[Describe the pictures on your plate.]* I like chicken. This is a drumstick. Here are some mashed potatoes. I also love chocolate chip cookies.

I made this plate to remind us that God gives us our favorite foods often. I am very thankful that I live in a place where I can have my favorite foods. Thank you, God. We have Thanksgiving Day to remind us to say thank you to God instead of just enjoying our favorite foods without being thankful for them.

Is anyone thankful for more than our food? Yes, you are happy for your parents. I am happy for my family. Without my husband and children, I would be very lonely. We have fun together. I love to have my grandchildren visit. You would miss your parents very much if they were gone. You would even miss your brothers and sisters. God gave them to us. Thank you, God.

We are also thankful for our houses. Homeless people live in cars or out on the streets. Sometimes they lie on the sidewalk and people walk around them. How sad. Thank you, God, for our warm houses.

God gives us even more! We have clothes to wear and washing machines to keep them clean. Did you know that in some countries people have to wash their clothes in a river? How would you like to do that? You don't even have to wash your own clothes! We also have more toys than we can play with and schools and cars and many, many more things. Thank you, God.

Let us say thank you to God for all the things he has given us that make us healthy and happy.

# 36

# Advent

**Object:** An Advent wreath

**Lesson:** The Advent wreath has special meaning for the Christmas season.

**Materials:** A piece of green construction paper, scissors, tape

**Project:** Make a paper wreath using green construction paper. Fold a piece of paper lengthwise twice (into long quarters). Then open the paper so that it is only folded in half. With the fold facing toward you, make cuts about a half inch apart that go up to the quarter fold. Do not cut to the edge. Open the paper and fold the two uncut edges over each other. Bend the ends of the paper in a circular manner until they touch. Tape the rounded shape together. The cuts from the center fold will fan out creating a wreath. Closer cuts will increase the fanned-out appearance.

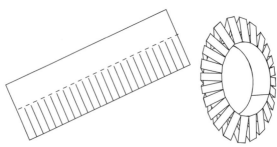

## Outline

*Introduce paper project:* Let's take a close look at this wreath I made.
1. The wreath is green because it stands for eternal life.
2. The wreath is round because it stands for the circle of love.
3. A real Advent wreath would have candles standing for the Christ child, hope, joy, peace, and love, which would be lit.

*Conclusion:* It will remind us of the true meaning of Christmas.


Let's take a close look at this wreath I made. It stands for many important things connected with the Christmas season. We call it an Advent wreath because we use it during the time called Advent, which leads up to Christmas, when Jesus was born.

This wreath is green. Real wreaths are made out of evergreen branches. They are green all winter and stand for eternal life. Eternal life means we will always, always live with God.

This wreath is round and has no beginning or ending. There is no beginning or ending to the love of God, which he shows us again this season with the celebration of the birth of his Son. God loves us; we love him. We love others; they love us. This love keeps going round and round.

A real Advent wreath would have five candles on it, one in the center for the Christ child and four around it for hope, joy, peace, and love, which would be lit during the Advent season. Candles are too dangerous for this paper wreath. We will use this wreath to remind us of the Advent season. It will remind us that Jesus brings us hope, joy, peace, and love. It will remind us of the true meaning of Christmas.

# 37
# Christmas

**Object:** A manger

**Lesson:** Jesus was born for you.

**Materials:** Brown or manila construction paper, ruler, pencil, scissors

**Project:** Construct a paper manger. Use half of a nine-by-twelve-inch piece of brown or manila construction paper for the trough. Fold it lengthwise into a v shape. With the fold facing toward you, make a one-inch cut about an inch from both edges. Cut two two-and-a-half-inch squares for the legs and insert them into the cuts. Open the trough to a manger shape.

## Outline

*Introduce paper project:* Why is this manger important to us?

1. The manger was a comfortable place for Jesus.
2. The manger was strong and safe.
3. The manger was not in the crowded inn.

4. The manger was not a rich, fancy bed. It was a common place.

*Conclusion:* He was born for all of us.

Why is this manger important to us? When Jesus was born, his parents put him in a manger for a bed. The manger was filled with soft hay, and the baby was wrapped in blankets. He was comfortable. God was taking care of him.

The manger in which Jesus slept was not made of paper. It was made from sturdy wood or perhaps even carved out of stone. It would have been strong enough so that the animals could not knock it over as they munched on the hay. God provided a safe place for Jesus.

Joseph and Mary really wanted to stay in the inn, which was where many travelers stayed. The inn was noisy and crowded. There would have been little privacy for a baby to be born and no room for the kind of special visitors who came to see Jesus on his birth night. God provided a special place for Jesus.

The fact that Jesus was laid in a manger has special meaning. Jesus was not born into a rich or important family, nor did he have an expensive, fancy crib. He slept in a common place. He came for the common people. He had important things to do for everyone, not just the rich, privileged people. He was born for all of us.

**Sheryl Bruinsma** is a Springfield, Pennsylvania, teacher who has taught for over thirty years and recently earned her Ed.D. degree. This is her ninth object lesson book.